TABLE OF CONTENTS

Introduction

Preppers come from all walks of life, and they participate in prepping to various degrees, depending on what they would like to accomplish. Some within the community are focused on short term survival; they have a 72-hour kit, and they're hopeful that first responders and government agencies will have things returned to normal rather quickly after a disaster. Other preppers have put together survival plans that will give them the opportunity to withstand disasters that last weeks, months, or even years.

When it comes to emergency preparedness, more and more people are becoming interested in developing a survival plan and increasing their chances of making it through any type of disaster that happens their way. Some folks are just beginning to learn what it means to be prepared, while others have all but mastered the self-reliant lifestyle. There are preppers who live in apartments within urban sprawls, and there are preppers who live on a homestead that has been in the family for generations.

It really doesn't matter where you live, or what walk of life you come from, surviving a disaster scenario is the key component to developing a survival plan. That being said, there are several activities we can make part of our daily habits that will augment the plans we currently have in place.

Food production is one of the biggest concerns for preppers. The introduction of GMO's (Genetically Modified Organisms) to crops within the industrial food chain, is also a huge concern for most people who consider themselves preppers. Many believe that GMO's alter the crops they are used on, and scientific studies seem to support this claim; indicating that short and long term exposure to GMO crops may be harmful to humans. Several countries on the international scene have banned GMO crop cultivation, but the USA isn't one of them. You can get a head start on stocking your pantry by getting your hands on this **survival super food**.

In addition to GMO's, crops grown commercially for the US industrial food chain, are subject to being sprayed with potentially harmful pesticides/insecticides, which is also considered harmful for human consumption. Truth be told; none of us know what harmful activities might be taking place to the food that ends up being delivered to grocery store shelves. Most of us blindly place our trust, faith, and health in the hands of the industrial food chain complex, without knowing anything about it, and that could be a recipe for disaster. In fact, several of the leading causes of illness and death are linked directly to the industrial food chain; obesity, diabetes, cancer, and heart disease are just a few of the more prevalent diseases that have been traced back to the industrial food chain and the stuff we eat.

Making matters worse is the fact that the majority of us have zero crop cultivation skills; we can barely grow grass in the front yard, let alone a small farm full of healthy edibles. As a matter of fact, if it weren't for the industrial food chain, most of us would starve off and die; we don't know how to grow food, forage for wild edibles, hunt, or fish. We have grown increasingly dependent on others to provide the sustenance we need in order to survive. While it may be necessary to stockpile food from the grocery store as part of your emergency preparedness survival plan, this should not be the primary source of sustenance for those who want to become self-reliant.

We are, quite literally, what we eat! Consumption of fresh healthy food often results in a fresh, healthy lifestyle. Thankfully, we have a couple of options available to us when it comes to taking back control of our health and our lives, as well as those of our loved ones. None of us would knowingly feed our families toxic substances, would we? I didn't think so; however, if we continue to follow our friends and neighbors to the regional chain grocery stores, then that is exactly what we are doing. So, let's take a look at a few food production possibilities we can all take advantage of.

Local Farmer's Markets

As stated previously, some within the prepper spectrum live in urban areas. This makes growing a garden difficult at best. In many cases, even those who are able to grow container gardens, vertical gardens, herb gardens, etc., on their balcony, or in a window, still can't achieve enough food production to remain free of the industrial food chain. However, rather than shopping at a chain grocery store, folks in this category can begin shopping at local farmer's markets.

Farmer's Markets often fall into one of two categories; they are privately owned and operated, offering surplus produce and food products that they grew themselves on a family owned farm. Privately owned and operated markets may also offer surplus food from other local farmers who meet the standards established by the owner. Other farmer's markets are open to all farmers in the region; they simply rent out booths to farmers in the area who want to sell surplus food from their farm. These types of markets are often weekend events, setup on Friday and gone by Sunday evening. In most areas these are weekly events that occur in the same place every weekend on schedule.

In addition to Farmer's Markets, you can also take advantage of bulk food offers to build a stockpile of surplus survival food. However, before you go that route it would be wise to grab a **sample of the surplus survival food** you want to include in your emergency preparedness plan.

When it comes to choosing a farmer's market to shop at, do the research. Food labels in the US are convoluted at best; just because something is labelled "organic," doesn't mean it has been grown by the standards you assume fall within the "organic" definition. It is highly recommended you find a privately owned and operated farmer's market for best results. Get to know the farmer, get to know the farm, if possible; take matters into your own hands. Most owners/farmers will have no problem discussing how they cultivate crops, nor will they be offended by asking if you can get a firsthand look at their operation.

Those who have nothing to hide, will be more than happy to share valuable information with you; they want your business and they realize that in order to get it, they must be willing to provide proof of their claims to offer fresh food. Those who refuse to discuss details, or schedule visits to the farm for further research, are more than likely using something at the farm that they know will be a deal killer for them and their business; avoid these farmers and markets at all costs.

Shopping at a farmer's market owned and operated by a member of the community, also helps support the local economy, which is something that doesn't occur as often as it should in today's society. In fact, we have been trained over the past several decades to rely on the convenience of consumerism. Bulk food stores are commonplace in urban/suburban settings; not only can you buy GMO produced food, you can buy it by the boatload at a lower cost. Technology has also provided us with the ability to shop, bulk or otherwise, with the click of a mouse. Several websites on the internet now offer **bulk food kits** that can be delivered directly to your door; you don't even have to go to the local chain grocer anymore if you're "too busy" with life to be bothered with something as trivial as food.

Volunteering:

Depending on the circumstances, it may be possible for you to volunteer to work at a local farm. Farmers often hire seasonal help to plant, tend, and harvest crops. It would not be unheard of to establish a relationship that allows you to volunteer on the farm in your spare time, in exchange for compensation in the form of fresh, healthy food.

Volunteering can give you an inside look at how crop cultivation occurs. This information is invaluable. You can use it to grow small container gardens at home, or to help establish a local "Community Garden," that grows enough fresh food for participating residents in the neighborhood.

You might also consider establishing a relationship with an owner of a farmer's market that allows you to volunteer at the market itself, assisting customers and stocking shelves. This would also allow you to receive compensation in the form of food rather than money, which will also improve your eating habits, and therefore your health and lifestyle.

Buying in Bulk:

No, not from the chain grocers we mentioned previously, or from the online outlets that offer such a possibility, but from local farmers! If you really want to regain control of your health and lifestyle, as well as that of your loved ones, then you might want to consider buying fresh healthy produce from a local farmer in bulk.

Rather than purchase enough green beans, carrots, and peas to flesh out the weekly menu for your family, consider buying these items by the bushel. This will save you money on the purchase and provide for your family for several months, if not the entire year. Granted, you will have to develop additional skills, or already have them, before making this type of purchase decision, such as canning, dehydrating, and preserving food for future use.

In all honesty, this is an idea that deserves serious consideration. Not only will you be saving money on the food purchase, you'll be saving a great deal of money by not having to drive to and from the chain grocery store every week. Additionally, you will be learning valuable skills that can be passed down to future generations, which in turn may help ensure the survival of your family for several future generations.

Community Gardens

Establishing a "Community Garden," may be easier said than done, especially in an urban/suburban environment. Land use regulations may prevent the cultivation of crops within a given region. For instance, most land use regulations in urban environments stipulate that the land has been zoned for "Commercial Use," or "Industrial Use." This means that anything established on land within these zones must meet specific criteria, none of which supports food production/crop cultivation.

Prior to attempting to establish a "Community Garden," it is imperative that you speak with the local zoning board. Although the land in question may be currently zoned for commercial or industrial use, it is possible to have it rezoned in certain cases.

The information below is not to be considered the "complete" guide to getting a community garden started. It will however, provide valuable information for those who believe this is the answer to obtaining fresh, healthy food. Each idea provided may trigger additional questions or concerns, therefore we recommend choosing topics from the list(s) that pertain to your situation specifically.

Form a Committee:
> First and foremost, you need to determine whether or not the community/neighborhood has a need, and/or a desire, to grow a

community garden
➢ Secondly, you need to decide what the garden will contain; trees, flowers, shrubs, bushes, vegetables, or a combination/mixture of all
➢ Who will benefit from the garden; the elderly, children, the people of the neighborhood, only those who participate by volunteering time and effort, etc.
➢ Are there stipulations for participation in order to harvest food from the garden; if so, what are they?
➢ Organize, schedule, and lead a meeting of interested members
➢ Nominate and select a gardening guru; somebody who is skilled in all things gardening
➢ Form, organize, and establish additional committees, as well as their respective duties; Fund Raisers, Youth Activities, Builders & Planners, etc.
➢ Try to find a sponsor. Sponsorship of a community garden can be an extremely valuable asset. They can donate tools, land, fertilizers, seeds, soil additives, or they may simply write a check to be used for whatever is deemed necessary.

  ○ Non-profit organizations, such as churches, schools, and parks might be a great place to look for sponsors

➢ Determine whether or not the community garden will have a membership fee
➢ Establish and maintain lists of things that need to be done
➢ Locate a plot of land suitable for establishing a community garden
➢ Buy, or lease, the land from the owner, or establish an agreement that permits use of the land for the community garden
➢ Decide who will be the administrator, as well as who will be supervisors; there should be a bare minimum of 3 people involved
➢ Establish a contact tree of all members; this lets you make announcements without leaving anyone out of the loop
➢ Name the community garden

Site Selection:

➢   If you do not own the land in question, find out who does

➢   Research the site for a several days; ensure it receives at least 6 hours, if not more, of full sunlight. If you grow plants that require more shade than sunlight, this can be achieved by establishing planting programs that grow large plants in close proximity to smaller plants; the larger plants provide shade for the smaller plants

➢   Have a soil test conducted; the soil must have the right minerals and nutrients, or plants will not grow, or they may not produce sufficiently

➢   Check the local vicinity for access to water; without water available in close proximity, you will have to transport it, and in great quantity, which is not recommended.

➢   Attempt to sign a 3 year lease/land use agreement; this gives you enough time to modify the soil and get the garden producing as it should

➢   Check local records for previous activity on the land; it may have been contaminated at some point in the past and unable to grow healthy food

Site Prep:

➢   The first thing you need to do is clean the site; remove all debris

and till the soil
> Develop a blueprint for land use

  o Pathways throughout the garden
  o Where plots for plants will be located
  o Which plants will be grown in which plots; companion growing concepts apply
  o Where is water located
  o Where will the tool shed/admin building be located?
  o Where will the compost pile be stationed, etc.

> Accumulate resources; the more you can get for free, the less you have to buy. Beg for donations!
> Establish a volunteer schedule and ensure tasks get done in a timely fashion
> Schedule activities for each day in the community garden
> Mark plots with boundaries and string
> Erect a bulletin board at the entry of the garden for posting announcements; make sure it is weather proof
> Consider planting flowers, shrubs, bushes, and/or trees along the border; this will help promote goodwill with the community that isn't involved with the gardening concept

Organizing the Garden:
> Outline, establish, and enforce regulations for membership

  o Do members have to pay dues
  o Do they have to live in the neighborhood?
  o Do they have to meet specific criteria?

> Determine how plots within the garden will be assigned

  o By family
  o By seniority
  o By group needs

> If there are membership dues, establish and outline how those

funds are to be used; you must account for membership dues and provide information to the members

➢   Will the garden be handled through community effort, or through individual skill?

➢   Determine what happens when a member quits, or is expelled

       ○   If plots are individually tended by families, how will the next member be chosen

➢   Determine how the community garden will be protected from vandalism/theft

➢   Will members share tools of the trade, or will they be responsible for maintaining their own

➢   What rules govern the use of the garden, and how will you ensure they are enforced

➢   Determine whether or not the land being used should be purchased, if possible, from the owner to ensure growing food for generations

Liability Insurance:

Depending on the circumstances, the land owner may require public liability insurance to be obtained before a lease for land use is signed, or an agreement is authorized. That being said, most small insurance firms do not have the ability to provide coverage for community gardens, so you may need to look at those firms that are listed in the "Top 10" category for public liability insurance in order to obtain what is required.

Organizational Concerns & Considerations:
> Determine the purpose of each and every member
> Outline and describe what the short term, as well as long term goals are
> Determine and detail how decisions are to be made

> o Will all members have a voice, or just those serving in administrative roles

> How will new leaders be chosen

> o Will there be annual elections?
> o How will vacant seats be filled if/when a member quits, or decides they no longer want to be in an administrative position

> How will tasks and duties be assigned
> Who will determine whether tasks and duties have been completed
> How will new funding be raised

> o Membership dues
> o Community based activities

> Will the community garden become incorporated, or remain as a group/club?
> Consider establishing and maintaining bylaws in order to prevent problems between gardeners and non-participating neighbors

It bears stating once again; this is not to be considered a complete list of considerations for establishing a community garden, but it should give you plenty of information to get started and point you in the right direction for further discovery.

Limited Space Gardening Concepts

In this section we are going to briefly describe small space gardening solutions that are suitable for almost any environment. Urban/suburban residents may find this information very useful given the area they reside in. We will cover the 4 most commonly mentioned small space gardening concepts, but that doesn't mean these are the only available opportunities for those with limited space for food production.

Herb Gardens:

If you have never grown a plant before, then an herb garden is where we recommend you focus your attention for the time being. The reason for this recommendation is simple; herb gardens are the easiest way to learn how to grow plants successfully. All that is required is a splash of sunshine, a few drops of water, soil that promotes drainage, and a dash or two of fertilizer.

Most herbs favor full sunlight with temperatures below 90°F. They can be grown in the ground, or in containers placed near a window. Location is of the utmost importance when growing herbs, so pay particular attention to where the herb garden is placed. As a bare minimum, the herb garden should receive at least 4 hours of direct sunlight per day.

Herbs grown outdoors in the ground, requiring a 1 to 4 foot diameter per plant. The soil conditions are also an important factor. Soil needs to promote drainage regardless of where the plants are located. Compacted soil will not allow plants to grow; loose soil promotes healthy root growth, which in turn promotes healthy plant growth. Compost or fertilizer should also be added to the soil to increase drainage and provide food for the plants to consume.

Herb gardens prefer to be watered when the soil is dry to the touch. We recommend using a "finger test," to determine when the plants require water. Stick a finger into the soil, up to one knuckle deep. If the finger comes out dry and free of soil, then the plants require water. If the finger comes out with particles stuck to it, then the soil still contains moisture and the garden can probably wait another day before needing water. You do not want to overwater an herb garden. They are small, compact gardens with minimal soil; too much water and you will grow mud.

Harvesting herbs for the garden is fairly simple. Clip off the top 1/3rd of the plant's branches once the herb has grown 6-8" in height. Clip the plants close to an intersection, where branches grow off the main stem of the plant; this will help the herbs promote new growth quickly.

If growing an herb garden indoors, make sure each plant has a pot/container that is at least 8" in diameter. This will give the plant ample room to grow. Bear in mind that they may outgrow these smaller containers and require transplanting in order to produce at a higher, more successful rate.

For novice gardeners with little experience, purchasing an herb garden kit may not be a bad idea. For a small investment you can get your feet wet with the concept of gardening and use what you learn to expand your knowledge when growing larger plants.

Vertical Gardens:

When it comes to vertical gardens, the only limitation is your imagination. Vertical gardens are an excellent option for those who have limited horizontal space, such as apartment dwellers and urban residents. People who live in these environments usually do not have a lawn, or enough land available, to grow a traditional garden; however, they almost always have a wall or two that receive adequate sunlight on a daily basis.

Vertical gardens can be attached to a wall that receives enough sunlight to promote healthy plant growth, or they can be free standing, such as a trellis garden. The important factor to be concerned with is weight. Vertical gardens, when attached to walls, add weight to the wall; this can cause structural issues if the wall wasn't built to withstand the amount of weight you are adding to it. Depending on the size, and number of plants in the vertical garden, it may be necessary to have the wall inspected, and/or enhanced with additional support before a vertical garden is attached. A good rule of thumb is to have the wall inspected if your vertical garden is going to occupy more than 50% of the available space.

In addition to growing a surplus of healthy food, vertical gardens also provide several other benefits that often go overlooked. Scientific research has shown that living plants improve air quality naturally; so much so that "living walls," also referred to as "green walls," are a trend that has taken off recently.

The architectural world is busy designing building plans that incorporate outdoor "living walls" that will transform the urban landscape in years to come. The interior design world is busy designing indoor "green walls" that will ultimately transform the way we live, both socially as well as privately. Malls around the world are building indoor "green walls" to add aesthetic beauty to an otherwise dull environment. Office spaces are doing the same, and it won't be long before we start seeing them become a part of the traditional housing industry.

In addition to reducing carbon emissions and improving air quality, a vertical garden can also improve the insulation properties of the wall, reducing sound and retaining more heat. Having living plants in close proximity, around the home and workplace, has also been shown to increase personal productivity, while simultaneously decreasing symptoms commonly associated with stress, depression, and anxiety.

There are plenty of options available when it comes to vertical gardening. To try and list each and every different concept that falls under the "vertical gardening" umbrella would be unproductive. The main purpose of growing a vertical vegetable garden should be to provide an ample supply of fresh, healthy food that can supplement your traditional food plan. Obviously the more you can grow for yourself, the better, so it is our recommendation you look at several ideas and concepts in order to find the ones that will satisfy your needs.

Container Gardens:

Container gardens can encompass anything from a single pot, to a windowsill box, at least as far as the small scale versions go. Raised garden beds are basically container gardens on steroids, but those are for folks with ample property to establish them.

Herb gardens are another example of container gardens, which we mentioned earlier in the book, but that same concept can be applied to growing vegetables. A single, large pot can be used to grow anything from potato plants to fruit bearing trees; it simply depends on what you have the desire to put in them.

Container gardens are perfect for people who have very limited space, or who share what space they have with others, such as roommates. They do not take up much space and they are easy to move in the event they need to be relocated. This allows you to place them out in the sun during the day and bring them in at night, if necessary.

Container gardening is the same as any other type of gardening; it gets the name because the plants are always kept in containers from seed to bloom and harvest. The same techniques and supplies that are mentioned throughout this book, apply here; water, fertilizer, and soil that promotes adequate drainage.

The biggest concern to be aware of is the lack of space within the soil that the container is able to hold. Plants consume minerals and nutrients from the soil and gobble up space as the root system expands; this can cause the plant to become "root bound." This occurs when the root system for the plant replaces all available soil and begins to expand beyond the limits of the container itself. Containers that host "root bound" plants may begin to show signs of bulging, and/or cracking, as the plant reaches maturity. Root bound plants often look sick. They will begin to wilt and decay rather rapidly if they are not transplanted into fresh soil as soon as possible. If you're going to grow a container garden, then make sure you know how much room each plant's root system requires in order to reach a successful harvest.

Miniature Greenhouses:

Miniature greenhouses come in all sizes, shapes, and configurations. Prefabricated mini greenhouses are available for sale from a number of distributors, and there are DIY kits and designs all over the internet. Some are so small they can be carried by hand from one location to another. If you have a bay window in your house, and it receives adequate sunlight throughout the year, then you already have a mini greenhouse started, you just need to complete it in order to start growing food.

There are many reasons to consider mini greenhouses, regardless of any other type of gardening you're going to do. For traditional gardeners, and those who will be growing vegetables outside when the climate is right, the mini greenhouse can be used to get an early start on seed germination, or to grow sprouts from seeds on a continual basis. The mini greenhouse is also a useful item to have if you clone a lot of your plants; the high humidity levels will give the graft a better chance of growing its own root structure and surviving.

Mini greenhouses do require more maintenance and monitoring than their larger counterparts, as humidity levels do increase quite rapidly, along with temperature levels, which need to be regulated to prevent problems occurring with your plants.

The are no limits to the types of plants you can grow in a mini greenhouse. Once you master creating the proper microclimate, you can grow anything your heart desires.

Vegetable Gardening For Beginners

If you're just getting started with growing a traditional vegetable garden, then we strongly encourage you to start small; you can expand the boundaries of your garden, and the plants you choose to grow in it, once you've gained the knowledge and experience.

Growing your own garden full of healthy edibles can be a very rewarding and enjoyable experience. Good soil, good seed stock, and a few healthy transplants are all you need in order to get your garden started, but to truly become successful at growing a garden full of healthy, organic vegetables, you'll need to learn how to keep your plants healthy and hearty.

The Basics:

When it comes to organic gardening, the first thing you need to dig into is the dirt. You need to have good soil in order to grow healthy plants. The best way to maintain good soil is to "feed the dirt" itself, rather than feeding the plants that grow there. In other words, you need to add organic matter to the soil instead of dousing the plants with synthetic chemical fertilizers, and for good reason.

When synthetic chemical fertilizers are used in the garden, they eventually strip the soil of anything useful. This turns the soil into a lifeless medium that does little more than give the plants a place to anchor their roots, which provides no form of nutrition for the plants growing in it. All the natural microorganisms that were once present in the soil, are now gone, and they will not return until such a time as the use of synthetic fertilizers is discontinued.

While it is always a good idea to add certain minerals and nutrients to the soil from time to time, such as greensand, rock phosphate, and ag-lime, the best thing you can use to maintain a healthy soil structure is organic matter, compost to be more precise. If you're going to grow an organic vegetable garden, there should be a working compost pile in close proximity.

Organic material works wonders on the soil, improving fertility and structure, which in turn provides the perfect medium for growing healthy vegetables. Composted organic matter gives the plants in your garden a rich source of carbon and nitrogen, and in a perfect compost pile, these nutrients will be evenly balanced.

The Compost Pile:

Since we mentioned it already, and it is such a key component of growing a healthy organic vegetable garden, let's take a look at what we can add to the compost pile. Bear in mind that there needs to be a balancing act when adding to the compost pile; too many "dry/dead" ingredients and you will create a carbon rich compost pile, too many "wet/green" ingredients and you will create a nitrogen rich environment within the compost pile.

Composting organic material doesn't just benefits the soil and plants in your garden, it also reduces the amount of household waste you are responsible for disposing of. If you're currently paying for trash pick-up from a local service provider, you may see a reduction in your bill, or you may be able to strike a better deal for having your trash removed.

Before we get into the list of items that can be added to the compost pile, lets take a few moments to cover composting basics. Prior to adding anything to the compost pile, make it as small as you possibly can. Cut, shred, chop, or tear items into smaller pieces, especially if you're going to be using it for a vegetable garden, as this will speed up the decomposition of material and make the compost available for use quicker than if the material was simply dumped on top of the compost pile and mixed together with the material already there.

Your compost pile will require plenty of air and occasionally some water. We recommend turning the compost pile on a weekly basis with a rake, or a tumbler bin. This will aerate the organic material and allow for better decomposition. You also want to keep the pile moist as much as possible; it should have the feel of a damp wash rag. Spray the pile down with water if it feels too dry; turn it more frequently with a rake if it feels too damp. Now, let's look at the list of compostable items.

Kitchen Items:
> - Wax-less paper plates (used)
> - Cardboard containers; cereal, pasta, sandwich bag boxes, etc.
> - Expired cereal
> - Expired crackers
> - Paper towels
> - Paper towel rolls
> - Crumbs from snack food packages

- Expired pasta sauce
- Expired tomato paste
- Expired potato chips, tortilla chips included
- Expired bread, tortillas included
- Leftover rice
- Leftover pasta
- Counter-top crumbs
- Shredded brown paper bags
- Cardboard from pizza boxes
- Used paper napkins
- Expired dairy alternatives; soy milk, almond milk, etc.
- Used tea bags that are made from organic materials
- Tea leaves
- Used coffee filters
- Used coffee grounds
- Smashed egg shells
- Vegetable scraps
- Fruit scraps
- Used paper cupcake cups
- Used bamboo skewers
- Used toothpicks
- Expired beer or wine
- Expired jams, preserves, and jellies
- Expired cheese
- Used corks from wine bottles
- Expired edible seeds; sesame, sunflower, pumpkin, etc.
- Shells from peanuts
- Expired oatmeal
- Expired energy bars, protein bars included
- Expired pretzels
- Expired candy
- Expired herbs and spices
- Shells from all nuts except walnuts; walnut shells are toxic to most plants
- Popcorn kernels that are burnt or that didn't pop

Household & Yard Items:
> ➤ Sawdust from natural wood; does not include treated, stained, or painted lumber products
> ➤ Leaves raked up during the Fall
> ➤ Grass clippings from mowing, edging, lawn maintenance
> ➤ Ashes from wood burnt in the fireplace; does not include treated, stained, or painted lumber products
> ➤ Used potpourri that contains natural material; does not apply to synthetic material
> ➤ Decaying or dead flowers
> ➤ Decaying or dead houseplants
> ➤ Trimmings from other plants
> ➤ Old rope
> ➤ Old twine
> ➤ Burlap sacks
> ➤ Construction paper
> ➤ Junk mail (remove any plastic windows)
> ➤ Old newspapers

Office Items:
> ➤ Shredded paper from documents
> ➤ Shredded bills
> ➤ Shredded envelopes
> ➤ Shredded paper business cards; does not apply to glossy finished cards

Laundry Room Items:
> ➤ Old, worn out cotton clothing, torn into smaller pieces
> ➤ Old, worn out denim clothing, torn into smaller pieces
> ➤ Old, worn out wool clothing, torn into smaller pieces
> ➤ Dryer lint, provided it comes from natural fabrics and not synthetics
> ➤ Old, worn out cotton sheets, torn into smaller pieces
> ➤ Old, worn out cotton towels, torn into smaller pieces

Bathroom Items:

> Human urine
> Used cotton swabs
> Used cotton balls
> Old, worn out loofahs
> Cardboard toilet paper rolls
> Used facial tissues
> Nail clippings

Pet Supplies:
> Used newspapers from the bottom of pet cages; birds, lizards, snakes, etc.
> Feathers
> Fur from brushing/shedding
> Certain animal droppings; hamster, gerbil, rabbits, horses, goats, cows, etc.
> Expired dry dog/cat food; does not include wet food
> Expired fish pellets; does not include flakes
> Used animal bedding; alfalfa, hay, straw, etc.

Holiday Supplies:
> Cardboard tubes from wrapping paper
> Garlands made from natural materials
> Christmas trees; reduced to mulching chips
> Used paper table cloths
> Crepe paper products
> Smashed pumpkins
> Wreaths made from natural materials
> Used hay/straw bales from seasonal yard decorations

That rounds out the list of recommended compost pile products. This is not an all-inclusive list of items that can be placed in a compost pile, but it does provide a pretty good start. There's an old adage among gardeners when it comes to composting; "when in doubt, leave it out." You cannot harm your compost pile by leaving out material you are unsure of; however, you can cause problems with the compost pile by placing items in it that would be better disposed of elsewhere, such as cooked meat and animal lard. Things of this nature will emit an aroma during decomposition that will attract predatory animals to the pile; once that happens they will be damn hard to get rid of.

Space Efficiency:

While it is possible to grow a garden anywhere soil conditions permit, the location of your garden should be positioned to provide the best use and efficiency of the space available.

Your garden should be placed in an area where it will receive adequate amounts of sunlight throughout the day. Depending on where you live and the ambient air temperatures, you may want to incorporate companion growing, or ensure there is shade available to help keep the heat at bay. While most plants perform better with ample sunlight, some do prefer shade, and others prefer a balanced approach of sunlight and shade.

You'll also want to locate the garden near a source of water. Nothing will wear you out quicker than having to carry water over long distances to feed the garden. If you have a natural water source nearby, consider having it tested and using it to water the garden; this will reduce expenses on your bill from a traditional water service supplier.

Depending on where you live, your garden may also require frost protection. This can usually be accomplished by covering the plants with plastic, thus creating a makeshift greenhouse type environment that traps heat from the plants and keeps them from succumbing to frost/thaw cycles.

Remember to start small, especially if you are new to gardening. Most people like to envision growing an enormous garden capable of providing enough vegetables to sustain them throughout the year. While that is an ambitious endeavor and one you should strive to achieve, it shouldn't be tackled until you have the experience of growing a smaller garden successfully. Raised bed gardens are often recommended for beginning gardeners, as they are fairly easy to manage and maintain.

Unless you live on a homestead, or are thinking of buying acreage, then it is recommended that you consider using raised beds for your backyard gardens. Traditional gardens, such as gardens on farms that employ long rows for each type of plant, are not feasible for gardens that will occupy a backyard setting. Raised bed gardens maximize the efficient use of space available. There will be fewer rows of plants, fewer rows to walk between plants, and more square footage to use for the plants.

Raised beds also require much less effort to manage and maintain. Vegetables grown in a raised bed that is used to maximize space will provide more shade to the soil below, which will keep it cool and require you to water it less often. This also means there will be less weeding to contend with, as well as less mulch to be concerned with. In a nutshell, it means there will be less work for the inexperienced gardeners to focus on, thus helping prevent any problems that might arise from a traditional row style garden.

With raised bed gardens, you don't walk as much on the soil that the plants are being grown in. This will reduce soil compaction, which will help keep the soil aerated, and aerated soil provides a much better structure for the roots of plants to grow in.

Crop Rotation Considerations:

If you plan on growing a garden every year, then crop rotation is a very important factor to consider. When rotating crops, the schedule you apply to your garden should prevent a crop from being grown in the same bed more than once in a three-year span. This helps to ensure that the soil is not stripped of the same vital nutrients on a yearly basis. Crop rotation might also help prevent insect infestation and plant diseases.

Let technology be your friend when developing a crop rotation schedule, or calendar. Sow your seeds and tend to your garden, then when the plants start to grow, snap a few pics of the entire garden and save it to a "Gardening Folder." This will help you identify which plants you placed where in the garden the previous year and help you decide where to place plants the next year. Date this information and keep it for at least three years, as a reference if nothing else, because in most cases memory alone will not catalog events correctly.

Creating a Continuous Harvest Cycle:

Another way to maximize the use of space available is to implement sowing crops in succession. There really is no reason to get all of your plants in the garden directly after the final frost of the season. Take a look at the zone you live in and determine when the best time to plant certain crops, then use this to your advantage.

Plant a new crop in the garden on a bi-weekly, or weekly basis. Hardy greens and snap peas can be introduced to the garden in the late winter/early spring seasons. Peppers and tomatoes can be introduced to the garden once the weather has reached steady warm temperatures. Finally, you can introduce frost hardy plant varieties in the middle of summer/fall seasons.

You can even introduce fast growing crops to the garden and replace them with other fast growing crops once they've been harvested. As a matter of fact, if you're going to grow a garden, then creating a continuous harvest cycle will be more beneficial in the long run.

Every time you get ready to harvest a crop, you should already have a replacement crop picked out and ready to grow. Start germinating the seeds for the next crop approximately 2 weeks before harvesting the existing crop. This way you can harvest one and transplant the other, all in a day's work, thus reducing the amount of time you need to spend tending the garden.

If you have several fast growing vegetable varieties, then you might even choose to grow them one behind the other. For instance, if you have a few radish plants in the garden, and you want to grow more, then as soon as you harvest the existing plant, replace it with a radish transplant that is ready to grow. This will allow you to continue growing and harvesting that variety of plant as long as the weather permits.

Maintaining Records

Although we mentioned this earlier, it bears repeating. Keep accurate records of everything you do, from one season to the next. This will help you determine what is and isn't working for you and your garden. You may find that growing a certain crop next to another crop causes both to have reduced production. You might also find that the opposite is true, certain plants grown in close proximity might actually benefit from the pairing. This is valuable information that can help you become more successful in the garden every year.

Your records can also contain the advice of seasoned gardeners. Valuable information of this type can help you identify problems you're having, what is causing the issue, as well as how to fix or repair the problem, and it might even assist you with preventing similar issues in future gardening projects.

We highly recommend having a small pocket notebook and pen/pencil available with you every time you're in the garden. Jot down dates and times for feeding, adding compost, watering, weeding, harvesting, transplanting, etc. This will help you master gardening over the course of time, and will more than likely teach you more about what goes on in a garden than any guidebook, or instruction manual, as those are normally written by people who aren't growing the same vegetables you are, or in the same soil conditions, limited space areas, etc.

It would also be wise to contact the local agricultural extension for the region you live in. They keep records of which plants perform best for the area and soil conditions present. They also keep accurate records of weather, which may come in handy for determining when to put plants in the ground.

Top 10 Plants For Novice Gardeners

If you're an inexperienced gardener, then you want to be successful with your first gardening experience, otherwise you may become distraught and give up on growing a garden the following year. With that in mind, we have assembled a list of the 10 easiest vegetable plants to place in your first garden.

Tomatoes:
- ➤ Start seeds indoors 6-8 weeks before the final spring frost
- ➤ Plant in an area that receives at least 6 hours of sunlight on a daily basis
- ➤ Harden transplants for at least one week before transplanting outdoors
- ➤ Introduce to the garden once the final frost has passed
- ➤ Stake tomato plants to prevent fruit from laying on soil
- ➤ Give tomato plants a two foot radius in the garden
- ➤ Water and tend pants until harvest

Zucchini & Squash:
- ➤ Start seeds indoors 2-4 weeks before final spring frost

➢ Plant in an area that receives ample sunlight throughout the day

➢ Introduce to the garden when the soil has reached a day time temp of at least 60°F

➢ Give squash and zucchini plants a two to three foot radius in the garden

➢ Water frequently and add compost when needed as these plants are voracious eaters

➢ Tend to plants until harvest

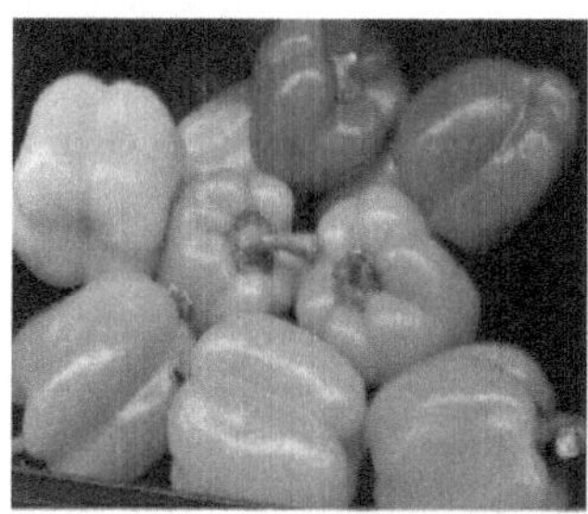

Bell Peppers:

➢ Start seeds indoors approximately 8-10 weeks before final spring frost

➢ Plant in an area that receives ample sunlight throughout the day

➢ Introduce to the garden when soil temperatures have reached 65°F

➢ Give bell pepper plants 18-24 inches of radius to grow in the garden

➢ Water and tend plants until harvest

Cabbages:

➢ Start seeds indoors 6-8 weeks before the final spring frost

➢ Harden off plants for one week prior to transplanting

> ➢ Introduce to the garden 2-3 weeks before the final spring frost
> ➢ Give cabbages 12-24 inches of radius to grow in the garden
> ➢ Water, feed and tend until harvest

Green Beans:

> ➢ Green beans are a harvested from climbing vines that can reach 15 feet in height
> ➢ Sow seeds directly into the soil after final spring frost; do not germinate seeds indoors
> ➢ Introduce to the garden when soil temps reach at least 50°F
> ➢ Stake plants and provide a trellis for vines to climb
> ➢ Sow bean seeds every 2-3 weeks for a continuous harvest cycle
> ➢ Water, feed, and tend until harvest

Lettuce:

> ➢ Seeds can be started indoors 4-6 weeks before final spring frost, or the can be sown directly into the soil once it can be tilled
> ➢ Harden off plants for one week before adding to garden
> ➢ Introduce to garden 2 weeks prior, to two weeks after, final spring frost
> ➢ Give lettuce plants approximately 12-15 inches of space to grow
> ➢ Water, feed, and tend plants until harvest

Beets:

- ➤ Do not germinate seeds indoors
- ➤ Direct sow seeds into soil once it reaches an average temperature of at least 50°F
- ➤ Give beet plants 1-2 inches of space in the garden to grow
- ➤ Plant seeds 20 days apart to add this plant to a continuous harvest cycle
- ➤ Water, feed, and tend until harvest

Carrots:

- ➤ Sow seeds directly into soil approximately 3-5 weeks before final spring frost
- ➤ Plant in an area that receives full sunlight throughout the day
- ➤ Give carrots approximately 3-4 inches of space to grow in the garden
- ➤ Water, feed, and tend plants until harvest

Swiss Chard:

➢ Sow seeds directly into soil 2-3 weeks before the final spring frost

➢ Plant seeds on a 10 day interval to add them to a continuous harvest cycle

➢ Give Swiss Chard plants approximately 10-20 inches of space to grow in the garden

➢ Water, feed, and tend until harvest

Radishes:

➢ Sow seeds directly into soil approximately 4-6 weeks before the final spring frost

➢ Plant in an area that receives full sunlight throughout the day

➢ Plant seeds on a two week interval to add them to a continuous harvest cycle

➢ Give radish plants approximately 2 inches of space to grow in the garden

➢ Water, feed, and tend until harvest

Marigolds:
- ➤ Plant in an area that receives full sunlight throughout the day
- ➤ Sow seeds directly into soil once warm temperatures arrive
- ➤ Give marigolds approximately 10-12 inches of space to grow in the garden
- ➤ Water, feed, and tend throughout the year
- ➤ Marigolds provide natural pest control and add a splash of color to the garden area

This completes the list of Top 10 plants for novice gardeners to consider. One of the topics we didn't cover in this book involves the use of tools and equipment. Depending on the type of garden, the amount of plants in the garden, and the land that is being worked as a garden, the list of tools and equipment will vary greatly.

People who are growing container gardens in pots will only need small hand tools, whereas those workin on vertical gardens may need a few more tools due to the nature of the environment and plants they are working with. Those who are going with raised garden beds, and/or traditional row gardening, will obviously require more tools and equipment than the others.

This guidebook is not intended to cover all aspects of gardening. There are far too many variables involved to provide accurate guidance to all readers; there are 13 different gardening zones in the US, separated into "a/b" sub zones, for a grand total of 26 hardiness zones.

This guidebook is intended to provide quick reference information for the novice gardener. The plants listed here are among the easiest to grow successfully, even for first time gardeners. However, the primary goal of growing a garden is to provide enough healthy organic edibles for you and